Information Security Breaches

Avoidance and Treatment based on ISO27001

Information Security Breaches

Avoidance and Treatment based on ISO27001

MICHAEL KRAUSZ

IT Governance Publishing

IT Governance Publishing
IT Governance Limited
Unit 3, Clive Court
Bartholomew's Walk
Cambridgeshire Business Park
Ely
Cambridgeshire
CB7 4EA
United Kingdom
www.itgovernance.co.uk

First published in the United Kingdom in 2009
by IT Governance Publishing.

ISBN 978-1-84928-115-7

Second edition published in in 2014
ISBN 978-1-84928-583-4

FOREWORD

In 1992, a business acquaintance of mine introduced me to something he called 'the ultimate book on information security'. It turned out to be a guide written by a retired NSA officer with a tendency to talk a little bit more than would probably have been allowed in the terms of the NDAs he had once signed. This, of course, was all the more appreciated by those listening to him. The book focused entirely on written information, and had originally been published in the late eighties or early nineties, a time when I started to use punch cards as notepaper because there was no longer any other use for them. Much as I respected the retired NSA officer, I felt uncomfortable because the book, even though it was only about 20 years old then, was hopelessly outdated and old fashioned. The way of working with information had changed so much since the time it was written that, early on in my career, I felt that I had to look elsewhere for guidance than to retired NSA officers.

Nowadays, with the ISO27000 family, general information and guidance on how to establish and preserve information security (IS) are readily available for purchase. This is not quite the case when it comes to the question of what to do 'if something happens'. Feeling that the market is not properly served, I thought that it would be valuable to provide the readership with insights on how cyber-investigations are conducted, and on what to do in the event of an incident. This guide aims to go right to the heart of what needs to be discussed, carried out and learned from an information security incident, covering the full breadth of issues that arise when the worst comes to the worst.

This guide is aimed at CSOs, CISOs, IT Security Managers, CIOs and, last but not least, CEOs. It particularly addresses personnel in non-IT roles, in an effort to make this unwieldy subject more comprehensible to those who, in a worst-case scenario, will be on the receiving end of requests for six- or seven-figure excess budgets to cope with severe incidents.

PREFACE

This pocket guide is intended to serve two purposes.

Firstly, it provides a general discussion of what information security breaches are, how they can be treated, and what ISO27001 offers in that respect, illustrated with details of real-life information security incidents. It aims to serve as a facilitator to widen the horizon of the reader seeking knowledge, or as an introduction for those who are just starting to think about information security.

Secondly, it will form a first line of defence for the reader who is the victim of an incident and is looking for guidance and direction. Here, it will help the reader by identifying, discussing and evaluating treatment options and, through the case studies, it will reduce the tension of the situation readers may find themselves in once a breach occurs.

This edition has been updated to be aligned with the 2013 update of ISO27001 (ISO/IEC 27001:2013). Prior versions were based on ISO/IEC 27001:2005.

ABOUT THE AUTHOR

Michael Krausz studied physics, computer science and law at the University of Technology in Vienna, and at Vienna and Webster universities. In order to combine his two main hobbies, namely investigations and computers, he has, over the last 20 years, become an accomplished professional investigator and IT expert. Since the beginning of his career, he has investigated over a hundred cases of information security breaches, usually connected with varying degrees of white-collar crime.

He has delivered over 5,000 hours of professional and academic training, and has provided services in 11 countries to date.

ACKNOWLEDGEMENTS

I gratefully acknowledge the assistance of IT Governance Ltd, without whom this book would not have seen the light of the bookshelf, real or virtual. In addition, the direct or indirect support
of friends, colleagues and business partners was very helpful.

CONTENTS

INTRODUCTION

Although breaches of information security are not a new phenomenon, the methods used to perpetrate such breaches have changed considerably over the years. Leaking information to non-authorised people has always been an issue but, in the computer age, the speed and effectiveness with which breaches of information security can occur, and the amount of harm potentially caused, are disturbing. Typically, also, they favour the perpetrator, not the victim.

Modern companies depend on their IT systems, and it is clear that special care needs to be taken to keep systems safe and secure. In this guide, we focus solely on the aspects of re-establishing that safety and security once, despite all measures taken, a breach has occurred. We put breaches of information security in the context of ISO27001 which, since its inception as former British Standard 7799 in the late eighties, has provided a framework of requirements well suited to the effective implementation of counter-measures and measures designed to protect information in all its forms (whether on paper, in the spoken word, or within the IT sphere).

This pocket guide outlines a process and its elements for the treatment of severe breaches, and places them in the context of the associated ISO27001 controls. It provides input for decision making and breach classification, and case studies where the reader can check out how other companies were affected and what they did, or did not do, upon becoming the victim of a breach.

CHAPTER 1: WHAT CONSTITUTES A BREACH?

Defining what constitutes a breach of information is not easy. Does only criminal activity constitute a breach? Is it only the things we read and hear about in the media, (such as the Army 'losing' data) or does everything that causes damage count as a breach? These are practical questions, even though they may sound strange at first.

When establishing the roles, responsibilities, processes and technologies required in a company to assure information security, these questions can be answered with ease at the technical level. They start to become more complex once the differing views of affected departments come to light; and the situation is aggravated when the parties involved lose focus and start playing politics instead of trying to solve the issues at hand. The bigger the company, the more likely this is to happen.

It is therefore important to provide a definition, or a working set of definitions, for use as the basis for consensus in a company.

The term 'breach' is not actually defined in the ISO27001 family. What is defined, though, is the term 'incident', as:

Information security incident[1]

[A] single or a series of unwanted or unexpected information security events that have a significant probability of compromising business operations and threatening information security.

Let us look in more detail at some of the phrases in this definition.

A single or a series...

---

[1] ISO27000:2012, page 5, paragraph 2.32.

The Standard acknowledges that, when something adverse happens, one single incident can be as damaging as a series of events.

The Standard does not provide guidance in regard to the number of incidents or the timeframe in which they occur. You need to establish this yourself, assuring that your company's specific requirements are met. The larger the company, the easier it will be to set up a formal regime of timeline and number thresholds. Ideally, you would set up a classification scheme which would provide an answer based on the number, timeframe and expected severity of the event.

...significant probability of compromising...

Do not be fooled – probability does not help in an adverse situation. Probability and statistics as a whole tend to be unsuitable tools for incident-related business decisions. You need to assess the impact of the event on your business operations. To do this, you will need to review technical and business processes, contracts and maybe criminal and civil law, as well as external factors, such as the public's reaction, media coverage, and so on.

Using the word 'probability' about an incident does not make much sense, as it suggests that there is a level at which no harm is done at all. Furthermore, it tends to provide a false sense of security. Instead, a thorough and dispassionate evaluation and the results of your incident-related deliberations are far more likely to give you an accurate picture of the situation.

To clarify matters, and as a starting point, let us briefly consider what constitutes information security. According to ISO27001, information security consists of ensuring the *confidentiality*, the *availability* and the *integrity* of information, as well as any other pillars that the company has decided to include, such as *non-repudiation*.

This means that any event which adversely affects the level of service of the processes charged with preserving confidentiality, availability or integrity (or whatever other pillars have been chosen) should be considered a breach. This is a good first thought when establishing the processes dealing with incident handling for your Information Security Management System (ISMS).

In other words, a breach can be defined as one of the following:

- a confidentiality breach
- an availability breach
- an integrity breach.

Confidentiality breach

A breach of confidentiality occurs every time the need-to-know principle, on which all dissemination of information should be based, is violated. Please note that the breach does not occur when the damage becomes visible, it occurs at the point in time when the company's guidelines have been violated. This difference is important, as it illustrates that the true point in time of a breach may be hard to determine, since a breach can take place in writing using a covert channel, by oral transmission or by electronic means including eavesdropping.

Availability breach

A breach of availability occurs when the Service Level Agreements that are in place are not adhered to, quite independently of any actual damage that may or may not result.

Calling this a breach is a little sharp, but it makes the point. In practical terms, one would only consider low availability a breach or an incident if it led to severe damage according to the company's definition of 'severe'.

Integrity breach

An integrity breach occurs whenever the integrity of information or its means of storage are violated, for example, by transmission errors, by intentional manipulation, by unintentional handling errors, or by corruption of file content or structure due to electrical, magnetic or other failures.

The definitions above are too broad and too inclusive. To narrow them down for practical purposes, we can establish that a breach has three dimensions of characteristics which, jointly, incorporate all the aspects required for treatment:

- impact
- source
- general treatment options.

Impact

Impact deals with what the incident is capable of causing. Will it only affect the company in a minor way (perhaps a server outage of not more than five minutes) or will it cause irreparable damage to the operations and the reputation of the company? Or will its effect be somewhere between the two? Can it affect the stock price of the company?

You need to set up a clear, non-overlapping set of levels of impact that should be aligned along the lines of:

- purely financial impact
- reputational impact – world
- reputational impact – customers
- legal impact.

It is important to make these distinctions, as these categories are not necessarily connected and can materialise alone or jointly.

A purely financial impact would result from an incident where money alone is sufficient as a remedy, such as a defective power supply that caused a server outage.

The difference between 'reputational impact – world' and 'reputational impact – customers' is made because these two target groups are not necessarily connected and communication with these groups usually differs in many aspects.

Take the defence sector, for example. It does not communicate with the public by banners in football stadiums or large advert campaigns, and its business is independent of the public mood.

On the other hand, insurance or tobacco companies and online betting sites communicate heavily with the general public which is their customer base.

A known breach of information security would therefore have a different effect on the remedial actions required by each of these sectors.

Source

What you can do about an incident depends on where the source is. Incidents can have multiple sources and sometimes the source (or 'root cause' as the ISO9000 community would call it) will only come to light after thorough investigation.

Potential source categories to consider are:

- external vs. internal
- unintentional vs. intentional
- manual vs. automatic
- human vs. nature.

External vs. internal

External refers to all sources which are not part of the company. *Internal* refers only to employees (those with a contract of employment) whereas all others, including freelancers, quasi-permanent freelancers, temporary workers, other companies, customers and suppliers are external. The difference is important, as the means of incident management are distinctly different. An employee can easily be interviewed about his role in an incident, while it might not be so easy in the case of externals or contractors, who might simply refuse solely on legal grounds.

At the same time, it is odd that externals can be more easily made to cooperate than employees, because employees have stricter contracts under the relevant labour laws. In most countries, these laws require the employee to demonstrate a level of trustworthiness which is not required from general business partners. Indeed, based solely on common law, a business contract cannot usually be terminated on the grounds of a lack of trustworthiness, which is why this is explicitly included in some cooperation contracts.

The bottom line is that the points below will decide the chances of success, should force or pressure be required to ensure cooperation in solving a case.

- The level of dependency on the business relationship or employment.
- The number of people involved, independent of whether the breach was of a criminal nature or the result of negligence or lack of training. The higher the number here, the more difficult it will be to crack the 'network'.
- The options that you can provide to the human source to come forward with the truth. A human with a lot to lose will, quite naturally, try to avoid cooperation, to destroy evidence and to resist interviews until there is no alternative.

Unintentional vs. intentional

Unintentional incidents usually point to one of the following:

A lack of training. This should be immediately remedied by appropriate training, and is one of the cases where an unwillingness to spend money up front (by providing the training in the first place) can have a disproportionately negative effect.

A lack of experience. This makes it necessary to replace the employee or employees at fault with more experienced ones.

A process irregularity. The process must be made clearer, easier to understand, or generally more accessible.

Technical deficiency of a software product. Changes must be made to the product's human interface or its deeper technical characteristics. You need to ensure that, especially when it comes to critical infrastructures, the systems should allow easy human interaction otherwise they will be risk prone.

Intentional incidents, however, usually occur simply because someone found that the results of the incident improved their life, or provided some worthwhile advantage. This applies equally to the banker who steals millions from customer accounts, to the teenager who tries to sell company data for a quick buck, or to the spy who steals data, as well as to politically motivated hackers who want to express an opinion by bringing down websites containing views to which they are opposed.

A proactive program to prevent incidents from occurring should ask the following questions:

- What is our level of exposure to malevolent groups of people? Who may want to harm us?

The usual suspects include disgruntled employees, greedy high- and medium-level managers, and employees who are short of cash as a result of poor personal decisions.

- How would they try to harm us?

For example, by denial of service attacks, by trying to damage our reputation or by bribery.

Developing answers to these questions best suited to your company and its specific market situation will greatly help you to decide on the specific measures you need to implement.

Manual vs. automatic

If the source of a breach was *manual* action, then the way to prohibit the same breach from happening again may differ from a situation where the source of the breach resulted from a malfunction of an *automatic* process. In the latter case, the breach will result in changes to the system, be it a process or a specific software program whereas, in the manual case, it may be advisable to replace manual process steps with automatic ones or to strengthen training.

Human vs. nature

The recurrence of breaches and incidents whose root cause was *human* actions can be prevented by replacing the human element with a computerised version of the same task, or by improving the training provided to the human in carrying out the task that caused the breach. Where the breach was intentional, of course, removing the human entirely from the situation is the more effective remedy.

If *nature* was to blame for the incident, such as a flood, an earthquake or a lightning strike, preventing the same type of incident from recurring tends to be much harder and more costly. In the case of floods, for example, flood gates might not be enough – you might have to relocate the entire company.

General treatment options

When dealing with incidents and breaches, the following dimensions of treatment exist:

- none
- internal investigation
- external investigation
- joint task force.

None

There are situations in which there are no options for treatment, or where the investigation has to stop at a certain point, either for lack of further facts or because of company politics.

It is rare that nothing can be done about an incident or about preventing it from recurring. Careful consideration of root causes can provide limited success in such situations, but it is likely that you will run out of options quite early on in the investigation; for instance, where the perpetrator has hidden in a foreign country where there is weak legislation, or where the company ought to relocate following a flood, but is not able to do so. In such cases it is still important to have documented all your deliberations, so that you can explain to an external tax auditor or a court of law why an investigative operation was stopped, or why no further measures were put in place.

Internal investigation

The staff involved in an internal investigation should include a leader, knowledgeable about techniques of investigation and capable of guiding people; strong social skills are recommended to keep the investigation on track.

Depending on the size of the incident, someone will be needed to track activities and produce, and retain, records of activity so that lessons may be learned from the investigation.

You will also require a number of technical experts. In larger incidents, the following is a good starting point: someone who knows about networks and network protocols; an operating systems expert, or even one expert per operating system involved; an application-level expert if applications are involved – for example, someone who knows about the inner workings of the SAP implementation in the specific environment.

A typical team would consist of three people for small incidents, and up to a dozen members for larger cases.

Courts of law have their own rules in regard to preservation and evaluation of evidence, among many other aspects. Once it has been established, therefore, that the incident will end up in court, additional experienced personnel should be included to provide continuous quality feedback on the investigation, and for review, to ensure that the best possible decisions have been made.

Breaches are not forgiving when it comes to mistakes made in the investigation. Small mistakes have the potential to lead the investigation in the wrong direction or, indeed, to invalidate the entire process.

External investigation

Some cases should not be handled internally due to the sensitivity of the subject. In general, every severe breach involving an employee should be handled under the leadership of external investigators as they tend to uncover the truth more quickly. The team needs the support of internal staff in getting to know the organisational structure and technical aspects of affected systems, but it will enact all measures independently and with the approval of senior management. External investigators should also be called, if a matter is too politically sensitive to be dealt with by internal staff.

Joint task force

A joint task force of internals and externals will only be required if the incident threatens the existence of the company or if the company simply cannot provide the know-how required from its internal resources. A typical joint task force would include the investigating team, a marketing communications expert or team, the affected department head, the CSO or CISO or another senior member of management, and the CFO, for ad hoc financial decisions.

Independent of the treatment option chosen, the investigating team needs to accomplish the results below.

- Find the root cause of the incident.
- Refine the root cause of the incident, for example, to a person, a technical system or a process weakness. There should be agreement in the team about the root cause, and differing opinions should be noted in the documentation.
- In cases of criminal actions, gather and follow up on the evidence as far as the investigation's budget will allow. The budget should be set up in advance and provide reasonable resources. The minimum is usually between £40,000 and £60,000 for larger cases, and can easily reach six figures.
- Clearly document constraints to the investigation itself.

CHAPTER 2: TREATMENT USING ISO27001

The following is an outline of a treatment process. It assumes as a starting point that the company has just been made aware, by internal or external sources, that a breach exists.

Assess the damage

This comprises the steps below.

- Assessing the immediate damage. Only material damage that has already happened is included.
- Assessing the long-term damage impact. Questions to ask: does this incident have a long-term impact, can it recur and does it have a systemic impact?
- Assessing the impact of the breach on business processes, your market situation, customer base, the public's reaction if applicable, and customer contracts. When assessing long-term damage, quite a bit of 'what-if-ing' is included. You should always balance potential damage with any mitigating circumstances in order to arrive at your conclusion.

Past or future?

This step consists of weighing the pros and cons of a deep investigation of the impact. ISO27001 requires your information security decision making to be sound and to be always based on the risk profile applicable to your situation. However, once a breach has materialised, it is only fair to ask whether it makes sense to investigate or whether the money would be better spent in finding methods of avoiding recurrence.

The heart of the matter here is how and what to set as the focus of remediating activity. Naturally, under no circumstances will ISO27001 allow you to just ignore the impact of the breach and continue as if nothing had happened.

Initiate an investigation, secure all evidence

This is mainly a technical task, relying heavily on a good level of documentation to find all the systems that are potentially involved.

In this step, you will identify affected systems and processes, secure material evidence, such as hard disks, and create disk images, storing them safely and securely.

Evaluate evidence

This is a step in itself, as time is absolutely critical when it comes to securing evidence. It is sometimes more advisable to secure all the evidence you can get your hands on, and do the evaluation at a later point in time than to do it all in one step. If the investigation is heavily IT-related, then securing the evidence before evaluating it should be the preferred method, as this is the only chance of winning the cat-and-mouse game with the hacker or perpetrator.

Draft the report

The incident report should contain the items below as minimum content.

- What happened, and when.
- What the root cause, or at least the suspected root cause, is.
- The timeline of who was informed and when they became involved in investigating the incident.
- All significant decisions regarding the case.
- The final case status achieved. Is it solved or unsolved, is the perpetrator known or still unknown, and so on.
- A summary of all follow-up action required, including suggested changes to processes.

Final decision

After everything relevant has been weighed, there should be a final decision of what the incident was about, what caused it, what the root cause was, and who the perpetrators were.

Follow up with tenacity

There is an afterlife with every breach. Once it has been resolved and all required measures have been identified, these measures should be put in place. Strangely enough, companies are sometimes quite reluctant, for all kinds of reasons, to implement identified measures. However, not following up on an incident is an invitation for it to recur.

Review

After a reasonable amount of time – this varies depending on the impact of the incident – a review should take place to check:

- if the follow-up was satisfactory and served its purpose
- if adopted pre-emptive measures have worked out as expected, and if they can remain effective under the given business environment.

The 'reasonable amount of time' can be one month, three months, or one year.

One year is usually enough to ensure that the incident and its associated measures are not forgotten, and to assess the long-term suitability of measures.

One month should be chosen for severe incidents that require immediate action. Within the company, this emphasises the importance of the measures being put in place.

Three months is a suitable amount of time for incidents of medium severity that do not merit a particularly harsh and disciplined response.

How ISO27001 supports the treatment of breaches

Of the 114 elements of ISO27001:2013, 15 deal with aspects that relate to the treatment of information security breaches. While breaches are directly addressed in only six of these, nine deal with aspects that should also be considered in choosing controls. We will discuss these elements in the order in which their control numbers appear in ISO27001.

Chapter 6 of the Standard, paragraph 6.1.1 and 6.1.2, sections a–e (see later) deals with the requirements for performing risk analysis, a precursor to incident handling as discussed in this guide.

A.6.1.3 – Contact with authorities

ISO27001 stipulates that your company should maintain ties with relevant authorities. This is not always feasible and, in some countries, it is even illegal. You should, therefore, maintain close ties where you can, and try to be as knowledgeable as possible about the general investigative processes employed by the authorities. This will help you conduct an investigation swiftly and without friction. Do not underestimate the effect of keeping informal ties, sometimes simply called 'knowing the right person'. While you should, under no circumstances, try to get favours from your contacts (as this might expose you to criminal charges) understanding each other's way of thinking considerably speeds up the flow of action. Additionally, the *modus operandi* of those criminals who have been apprehended has usually turned out to involve the use of shared knowledge; companies can gain considerable benefits from understanding how the criminal element tries to subvert their services.

A.7.2.2 – Information security awareness, education and training

The existence of an appropriate IS awareness programme is quite likely to stop incidents from occurring, and is essential in ensuring the right reaction to breaches. A good programme achieves the following:

- Short reaction times in reporting incidents to the right people through the right channels; 'right' in the sense of 'defined'.

- A general sense of direction in what to do when an incident occurs.
- Clear directions for disciplinary processes for those committing breaches that can lead, or have led, to incidents.

A.7.2.3 – Disciplinary process

This is a peripheral aspect of treating information security breaches, but it should be clearly communicated to employees what the personal consequences of breaches are. This is because, although there is disagreement as to whether the knowledge of such consequences acts as a deterrent, transparency can encourage cooperation. Knowing the penalties will also make the potential perpetrator's decision more difficult.

A.8.1.4 – Return of assets

It is surprising how often breaches are caused by information systems not being disposed of properly, or even not being returned to the company when an employee leaves. To name just two examples, such breaches include NATO laptops being found in flea markets, with target data of the war against Serbia, and federal ministry laptops being sold on eBay by an employee of the company that had been charged with disposing of the disks.

As a general rule, critical IT systems should be physically destroyed by the company itself. The use of third-party providers is justified in a large company (10,000+ employees) or if the data handled is particularly sensitive.

If your company does not belong in that category you should insist on your service provider being audited, either by you or by an IS auditing company, as such providers constitute a prime source of 'lost' data.

A.9.2.6 – Removal or adjustment of access rights

Access rights of former employees should be removed as soon as no longer required, to minimise the potential for abuse. Temporary workers, freelancers, and so on, also fall into the 'employee' category and should not be overlooked. Special care should be taken in regard to those freelancers or temporary workers who are 'semi-regular' and have non-contingent working assignments over an extended period of time. Their accounts should be locked when not in use to prohibit misuse by insiders or others.

A.12.2.1 – Controls against malware

Viruses and Trojans or APTs are a prime method used by attackers to get data out of a company. It must be ensured that the environment is free of viruses and Trojans, and that active measures are in place to combat root kits. If a company has lost data through theft, and the use of viruses cannot be ruled out, the investigation will become infinitely more difficult as it will be necessary to check for this potential source of the leak. If the source cannot be narrowed down to a team or department then, in the worst case, you could find yourself having to examine all the computers in your company, looking for viruses or Trojans.

You should also ensure that, in event of a successful virus attack, you have a defined recovery process in place to cleanse your systems of viruses, root kits, and so on. In practice, this means having disk images or other restore methods ready for redeployment on client or server machines. Good system documentation is also vital if you are to be able to recover speedily.

A.12.4.1 – Event logging

Having log files is an essential proactive means of security and incident resolution. Without logging there is simply no means available for investigators to delve into past events. The quality of what is logged – and the more, the better – determines its worth in an investigation.

A.12.4.2 – Protection of log information

If it has been tampered with or damaged, the worth of a log file can be greatly reduced or even lost completely. It is important to keep log files safe and secure by applying MD5 hashing, or by using other means, such as writing the files on one-time-write media, such as CDs or DVDs, to ensure that they cannot be tampered with once written. A smart perpetrator might try to lay a false trail by tampering with log files.

A.14.2.5 – Secure system engineering principles

This may seem a bit odd at first, but if your organisation is a software development company, then you should put principles in place to ensure secure system engineering. This will help prevent any consequences caused by a breach from affecting the software itself. It might even stop the breach from occurring, as the software will not be vulnerable to the specific technical pattern of attack.

If your company is more of a 'user' – only working with purchased software (off-the-shelf or customised) – then the software vendor's application of such principles will determine **your** susceptibility to a breach. This applies whether the software is public-facing or intranet-facing.

The following controls are those directly relevant to the treatment of information security breaches.

A.16.1.1 – Reporting information security events

This is a standard operating control stipulating that a process exists to report security events independent of their nature. While most events will be treated through standardised operational channels (for example, the team responsible for server or network operations) a substantial breach may first be noticed because of a comparatively minor event at a lower level. This control includes the reporting requirement for severe breaches and incidents. You should therefore ensure that a clear reporting process exists and that the parameters for categorising events are clear and understood by all those affected.

A.16.1.3 – Reporting security weaknesses

A weakness (as opposed to an event) is a condition a system is found to be in, for example, due to a lack of applied updates or patches. Although this refers primarily to technical weaknesses, sufficient management attention must also be directed at organisational weaknesses, which should be named as such. Consider, for example, whether a situation in which the four-eyes principle has not been applied also constitutes a weakness. (The four-eyes principle describes a procedure by which all actions carried out by one employee are verified by a second employee. This could happen at the time the action is carried out or – in some cases – at a later stage of a process.)

A.16.1.4, A.16.1.5 – Assessment of and decision on information security events / Response to information security incidents

These controls deal directly and indirectly with having clear procedures and responsibilities in place to assess and handle an event or incident. The line of thought followed in these controls is that many events may occur, but depending on your exposures, risk situation and the severity of the event it may or may not be an incident (dependent on the decision criteria you have set up for your organisation).

Nothing will act as a stronger impediment to an investigation than responsibilities and roles that are not clearly defined or, indeed, not defined at all. When a breach has occurred, swift action is required and everybody involved needs to be trained and clear about their roles and responsibilities. Otherwise, the investigation can deteriorate into an endless sequence of conflicts about the authority to execute each step.

A.16.1.6 – Learning from information security incidents

Once an incident has been contained or resolved it is vital, in the long run, that the lessons that can be learned are actually taken on board. Very occasionally, there is no lesson to be learned, but this is the exception, not the rule. The company must ensure that the outcome of this learning phase is implemented, whether in the form of additional training, new systems, or changes to existing systems or processes.

A.16.1.7 – Collection of evidence

ISO27001 stipulates that the company needs to know the rules applying to the collection of evidence in the jurisdictions in which it operates. This is vital. Not all companies may wish to take their breaches to court but, once you do, you need to have the assurance that the evidence collected throughout the investigation is admissible in court. If it is not, the situation will turn in another direction – against you.

It should be noted that international companies will first have to establish the number of jurisdictions they are exposed to, and then get proper legal support for all of them. Smaller companies may find it hard to gain full support at reasonable prices, and they therefore usually take higher risks. For the purposes of investigating breaches, at least being aware of such issues is half the battle.

In the remainder of this chapter we will present the basics of risk management as outlined by the Standard. Although risk management is peripheral to the subject of this guide, we felt it necessary to put our main subject in context. After all, an organisation's risk management should prevent the occurrence of incidents like the ones we are discussing.

6.1.1 and 6.1.2 a-e – Information security risk assessment

ISO27001 is all about risk management and minimising the risks to information processing systems and structures and to the organisation itself. This pocket guide comes into play once those minimisation techniques have failed, so it is well worth looking at what came before.

Chapter 6.1.1 defines in general terms that the organisation shall determine risks and opportunities to ensure that the entire ISMS can achieve its intended outcome (some of these might be internal risks such as lack of management commitment or funding, some will be external). It states that the organisation must have a plan to address these opportunities and risks (no specific risk management model is imposed on the organisation) and that the organisation must evaluate the effective measures taken to achieve this at a later date.

Chapter 6.1.2a of the Standard mandates that the organisation define a risk management process suited to its ISMS. Risk acceptance criteria and criteria (or a methodology) for performing information security risk assessments are defined.

Chapter 6.1.2b states that the methodology applied must be able to produce consistent, valid, and comparable results. This is essential in proving to management what the truth about the ISMS's effectiveness actually is and which parts of it perform well, show improvements or don't and for what reason.

While it is comparatively easy to achieve continuous improvement in a quality management system (ISO9001), an ISMS might still be effective even if certain events might at first suggest otherwise. For example, if a new type of virus or APT (Advanced Persistent Threat) appears it is clear that your organisation will be affected to a degree if attacked, but the speed and effectiveness with which you can detect and counteract the APT through the processes you have set up can show that your ISMS is still effective. So using the number of attacks you face as a measurement parameter might not be best choice, as the mere number does not show how well the threats are dealt with.

Chapter 6.1.2c, mandates that you apply the risk assessment process you have chosen to assess risks/consequences associated with the loss of confidentiality, integrity or availability of information (information assets) within the chosen scope of your ISMS.

It further mandates that you identify risk owners. They are roles within your organisation which include the responsibility to mitigate or at least document risks.

It is of paramount importance that these are the roles that can actually make informed decisions about the risk and have the means (resources) to tackle risk mitigation. It does not make sense to transfer all responsibility for understanding and mitigating risks to the CIO or system administrator in a complex organisation, unless they have the power to allocate resources to deal with threats or at least to isolate affected systems. What does make sense is to assign department heads or team leads as risk owners (provided they have a meaningful degree of budget authority).

In smaller companies these roles will be the IT manager and executive management.

Chapter 6.1.2d, mandates that risks should be analysed in terms of their potential consequences and realistic likelihood of occurrence, and that risk levels shall be determined.

It is very useful to start with threat identification and base this on publicly available threat catalogues, such as the German Baseline Protection Manual's catalogue (www.bsi.de). It contains some 500 threats that can be used to determine whether, and to what extent, your assets are vulnerable. Some companies offer threat catalogues containing up to 4,000 threats but at this level manual evaluation becomes cumbersome and quite long-winded.

To identify the impact of losses of confidentiality, integrity and availability you need to consider at least the three elements below.

- **Direct damage** to the assets (e.g. hardware replacement).
- **Process damage** caused by the failed asset. This means thinking about the entire process that the asset is part of, and determining the damage caused. For example, a simple printer in an important place can bring down an entire logistics chain if it fails.

- **Indirect process damage**. This relates to extending the view beyond the current process of which the asset is part, to all processes depending on this process. This type of damage is usually the most difficult and time-consuming to evaluate; it is, nevertheless, needed if you are to achieve a clear and true picture of damage potentially suffered.

By evaluating threats and if they can affect you at all (e.g. a Z/OS threat will not affect a Windows machine), and then considering both the likelihood and the potential impact on your information assets, you are migrating from a threat view to a risk view. Usually, it makes a lot of sense to start out with a matrix in which you place the threats on a scale of likelihood (3 to 5 levels) and impact (3 to 5 levels) thereby yielding risk levels within the matrix.

Chapter 6.2.1e deals with comparing the results of the risk analysis from 6.2.1d and comparing these to the risk criteria established in 6.1.2a. These criteria can be established along the lines of material damage that your organisation can afford or is willing to afford (which depends on your risk appetite) and additionally on non-material risk criteria such as reputational damage with customers or the general public.

Additionally, the chapter wants the organisation to prioritise the analysed risks, which can be done very effectively by comparing the risks in a matrix of risk level vs. mitigation cost. Clearly, you should begin by tackling those risks that are severe and can be mitigated easily (with only a little funding). Those that cannot be mitigated because the cost would exceed your means you will have to accept, whereas those that are of little relevance (independent of cost) you can simply ignore until your next risk analysis. All risks in between those cornerstones you can prioritise based on resource availability, which should not only include cost but also whether you have the people available to do it in the desired (or mandated, e.g. by customers) timeframe.

Whichever method you choose, as far as getting and keeping a certificate is concerned, you need to ensure that your method:

- is logically sound
- leads to sound business decisions about treating risks
- is evaluated yearly for its effectiveness
- actually reduces the risk level to which assets are exposed.

Finally, chapter 6.1.2 mandates that the organisation retains documented information about the risk assessment process in place. Not only is this essential in allowing organisational learning, you cannot get ISO27001 certified without this documentation in place.

CHAPTER 3: CASE STUDIES

This chapter is intended for the curious reader who would like to know about other companies' experiences with a serious incident, and the outcomes. Although ISO27001 stipulates that, to enable learning, companies should share information on such experiences, it is actually difficult for them to do so. Nobody likes to admit that they have had a serious problem. This is understandable as, nowadays, it is highly likely that customers, members of the public or even government officials will try to gain some windfall profit from such an incident through lawsuits, bad press or other action. In addition, of course, if the company affected is publicly traded, the stock market may react quite severely to news of a serious breach.

We have included four case studies in this pocket guide to illustrate the above points. They are ordered according to company size, to make the studies more accessible to the reader. An information security risk profile does not by any means depend on the size of the company. The larger a company, however, the more likely it is to recover fully from an incident. More precisely, it is the prudence of management that decides on a company's fate once a serious incident occurs, not only the size. A small company with lots of cash will certainly find it easier to undertake necessary action than a large company that has overdrawn its credit lines.

The case studies have been normalised and security-cleared to protect the innocent and (unfortunately) the not-so-innocent. All cases described took place in central Europe between 2000 and 2009.

Case study 1 – small company

On the importance of assuring availability

One summer morning, Peter B, the owner of a small but specialised computer repair business, the best-known one in a city (City X) of two million inhabitants, came to work and found the following:

- none of the three computers used for administering the shop would boot
- all customer and accounting records (paper) were gone
- his long-term employee, Alex D, did not show up for work and did not respond to telephone calls.

It was immediately clear that the month-long quarrels between Peter B and Alex D had turned very sour.

Worse still, it turned out that Alex D was about to open up his own business and had already approached old customers, stating that his prices would be much cheaper than those Peter B offered. That plan failed as, in this case, customers showed considerable loyalty once they had the full picture of what had happened. Such customer loyalty is exceptional, and cannot be included as a mitigating factor in a risk analysis because of its inherent unreliability. Alex D's repair shop actually went bankrupt after six months, following heavy price competition between the two shop owners.

On the IT side, the whole situation seems easy at first sight. The course of action would be to:

- get back-up tapes/disks
- reinstall computers
- restore back-ups.

That would certainly have been the case, had Peter B always been disciplined about his back-ups. Unfortunately, this had not been the case lately, so it took about three months to fully re-establish all his customer and accounting records.

The damage in this case was multiple and illustrates, on a comparatively small scale, the extent of such incidents.

- Where available, customer data had to be restored from delivery receipts, invoices, or simply by waiting for customers to complain that their repairs had not been finished on time; a tedious, manual process.
- Many customers needed to be contacted personally to re-establish basic facts, such as addresses, telephone numbers, and bank account data.

- The tax authorities had to be spoken to, to explain delays in VAT transfers which, in City X, are due monthly.
- Customers had to be convinced that normal operations would resume soon. Fear of potential loss of trust is an aggravating factor at this point in such cases.
- Peter B did, in fact lose some customers. Alex D's pricing presented Peter B with the challenge of getting customers back through other factors, such as service quality, or by matching Alex D's prices. This implicitly undermined Peter B's business model.

In the end, did Peter B sue Alex D for damages?

Actually, no, for the reasons outlined below.

- Alex D's behaviour in regard to the IT systems just did not count as a criminal offence at that point in time.
- What actually was a criminal offence, was the theft of customer data or, rather, the use of it to gain an unfair advantage. Peter B considered his chances of suing and came to the conclusion that, in this case, it simply wouldn't make sense. While his chances of winning a lawsuit were very good, Alex D would probably not be able to pay up, whatever the verdict.

Lessons learned

Back-up is of critical importance to any business depending on computers to render its services. Small companies have a tendency to underestimate this while, for medium-sized to large companies, the requirement for back-up is so obvious that it doesn't need discussion. Simple measures, such as keeping the back-up at home, would already have been enough to drastically reduce recovery time.

Legal action. For a small company, time is of the essence. This means coming to a decision about whether it is wiser to speed up recovery as much as you can, or to spend time in securing evidence

to go to court. Bluntly, for small companies (or indeed any company) with limited resources, it makes much more sense to look forward than to engage in an investigation. When Motorola and Intel, or Oracle and SAP, or Microsoft and IBM fight each other in court, the potential gain outweighs the cost by orders of magnitude, and the companies are not risking their entire existence. For Peter B, going to court would have been costly without any likelihood of recovering damages. It is not unusual for smaller companies find themselves caught in this sort of trap.

Case study 2 – small company

On data integrity – why you should use Word templates correctly

There was (and still is) a company that provides ISO9001 certification services for its customer base of 4,500. This company is a market leader in its country, somewhere in continental Europe. It has only about 40 employees at two sites, which actually makes it a small company by most definitions. It is, however, small only in employee numbers, not in revenue.

To keep costs low, the company does not employ its auditors. For most auditors, auditing is a second job after their main employment, unless they are working as freelancers. This can be quite disturbing when it comes to enacting remediating action after an incident.

The incident occurred as follows. A freelance auditor decided to cut corners and use one company's audit report as a template for the audit of another company. At the second company, the manager was quite surprised to find that another company's details appeared when he turned on change tracking in Microsoft Word. The call the auditing company's director had to face later that day cannot have been too pleasant.

This incident is a classic example of what happens most: unintentional breaches, caused by lack of training or experience.

The company manager, a person with 30 years' experience in his profession, did manage to re-establish trust with the affected customer quite soon, but the incident would have consequences for the whole staff of 400 freelance auditors. All were forced into changed agreements which stipulated that Word templates were only allowed to be used once per customer; that a new template had to be opened for each customer; and that under no circumstances was it permissible to send a Word file to a customer.

Lessons learned

The company was in a situation where it could not fully rely on an equal level of training for all its critical staff, as these were not employed at the company. Hence, a **legal framework** was needed to establish clear guidelines on what constituted expected behaviour in regard to information security.

It also became clear to the company that a **stricter regime** regarding information security was needed, so they hired an external expert to conduct an ISO27001 gap analysis and, eventually, decided to become certified.

Case study 3 – medium-sized company

The missing contracts

This case is not for the faint of heart, as it illustrates some of the rougher aspects of today's company life.

Four medium-sized, highly regarded companies decided to join forces and brands, and combine one aspect of their activities into a new company and brand. That company, henceforth called X, was established and one managing director (Y) was given full, sole decision-making power on all business aspects. He was given an assistant leased to company X by one of the mother companies.

At first, all went well, and company X performed well. Suddenly, however, managing director Y developed a deep-seated desire to get rid of one of the owners by having his assistant dig up enough dirt. Even today, nobody involved really understands what drove Y to that behaviour. So, after having run down company X, and after months and months of intrigue, Y was finally fired.

At this point, it turned out that Y also had to be fired a second time, by all four mother companies in joint agreement. He could not just be fired from company X. Naturally, his assistant was fired, too.

All now seemed well in company X until, one day, the assistant called to claim his termination settlement in accordance with the new employment contract that Y had agreed with him. However, no contract could be found. The assistant threatened legal action, but was willing to accept less, if the matter were promptly settled. Since no one at X could find that contract, the cards would favour the assistant, should he go to court. Additionally, the former managing director was claiming money and benefits according to a new contract which he had obviously agreed on with himself, a consequence, as it turned out later, of being given sole decision-making power. Again, that contract could not be found.

So, finally, an investigator was called in and was provided with the laptops of the former director and assistant. Although these laptops had already been reused, the investigator was able to fully recover both contracts. One minor detail turned out to be of utmost significance. Both contracts were created between Y's first and second firings.

The court of law concluded from this that, in a situation where Y was legally still employed but had obviously lost the trust of the owners, he would not have been allowed to enter into agreements that were not in line with the owners' best interest and which were blatantly against company practice. So the claims of both the former director and his assistant, totalling close to one million Euros in all, were rejected in all three courts of law. Needless to say, the company was relieved after the first verdict, but it would not have taken much, maybe just a few more weeks of use of the laptops, to destroy all chances of success. Legal action in this case was spread over a period of more than two years, as the two perpetrators used every opportunity to appeal a prior court's decision.

Lessons learned

When there is a breach, you must isolate the laptops (or the affected systems) right from the start. Continuing to use them reduces, by orders of magnitude, the chances of finding good evidence. In this case, the company was just plain lucky.

Do not hesitate to call in investigators. Company X took about three weeks before an investigator was called in, which exposed them to a lot of unnecessary stress and hassle.

Evidence needs to be secured professionally so that it holds up in court. In this case, the plaintiff did not question the evidence once presented, and the judge relied heavily in his verdict on the explanations of the investigator as expert witness.

Case study 4 – large company

Data theft – who wants my data?

There is a company (let's call it B) whose revenue relies solely on customers using its online (web-based) services. It has about two million regular customers and employs a small team purely for the purpose of reading Internet forums to assess what the customer base has to say about the company.

One day, one of the members of this team read something like this in one the forums that they monitored daily:

Do you want to start your own online business? Do you need a customer base? Customer data of company B for sale – full records available.

After an initial shock, the matter was quickly referred to the company security department that had been established only recently. They acted swiftly and immediately contacted an investigator to assist with the investigation by providing technical input, input on how to best conduct an investigation and on how to bring the perpetrator to justice. Action on two fronts followed, with the company trying to find out if, and how, data had actually left the company, and the investigator entering into fake negotiations with the seller to establish as many details as possible about him or her.

In such cases, the investigator usually has to purchase a sample of the data to verify whether the case has substance or whether it is just a fake. Someone could claim to have data, expect potential customers to pay in advance, and then simply defraud them of their money. In the cyber crime world that counts as a valid business model.

After a comparatively short time, it became clear that the data offered was authentic but incomplete (i.e. it was not data from the whole company but only from a specific business line). On the investigative front, the seller could actually be easily identified, as traces led to a website in whose source code a full name was included. Furthermore, the seller identified himself using the same full name, thereby establishing certainty, and the DNS records of the website pointed to a specified person with an address. An investigator's dream come true – all the facts were at hand.

In the next step, the investigator established informal contact with police to make sure the matter was handled discreetly and with prudence. After having established a working relationship, the investigator presented the case to the police team assigned and was quite surprised to find that the seller had already had one run-in with police. This was all the more surprising as the seller turned out to be only fourteen and a half years old, though still old enough to be prosecuted.

Legally, in this case, the seller could have been charged with illegal access based on computer crime law, and unfairly exploiting a trade secret in commercial law. However, it became clear that there was insufficient evidence to go for the computer crime offence and that suing for unfair exploitation of trade secrets would be very tedious when it came to customer data records, and not really promising. So the seller was finally charged with fraud, as it turned out that he had offered the entire customer base of company B, while only possessing a short file of sample records himself. For this he got a comparatively minor conviction and received probation, due to his age. He was also fully cooperative once caught.

The root cause turned out to be that company B had purchased another company some months earlier. Staff there had not properly removed a system from the Internet, leaving it open for use but no longer patching it. This made it possible for a perpetrator to download customer records. As the purchased company did not have any kind of structured, organised security in place, this went unnoticed until company B received its wake-up call by reading the monitored forums.

The actual perpetrator was never found. There was not enough evidence, because of a lack of logging, and because the interrogation of the seller did not shed much light on the people behind him.

Lessons learned

The lessons learned from this case are numerous and all relate very well to what ISO27001 suggests and mandates.

There needs to be a clear procedure for removing systems from operational use. In this case, that was the root cause of the matter.

There must be an incident management process to assure that the right people are speedily informed.

You should already have a working relationship with the local computer crime police unit, to exchange views on current threats and on the best way to proceed.

Systems need to support logging features. Without logging, your traces will go cold very soon, leaving you in the dark without any chance of being able to continue in a meaningful way.

If the breach is perpetrated from the outside and from another country, the entire case may take months and weeks to resolve, if at all, as – especially in Europe – inter-police cooperation cannot be taken for granted. In the USA, on the other hand, credit card fraud involving amounts of less than $150,000 is not even investigated, as such cases are deemed too small by the US Secret Service whose mission it is, among other things, to investigate credit card fraud.

Legal advice is needed to clearly identify which kind of behaviour can be followed up on and which cannot. This is clearly a challenge as, even in Europe and the USA, there is no common agreement on what is punishable and what is not, since not all countries have ratified the Cybercrime Convention, nor do they have comparable laws. The legal advice provided throughout an investigation will yield important input on how best to proceed to guard the company's interests.

The PR department of the company needs to be involved quite early in the process, to be able to prepare statements should such a case come to the attention of the public. Their staff need to be informed in clear words and without going into too much detail, as communication departments cannot be expected to fully grasp the extent of such a situation in technical terms.

As our case studies have shown, information security incidents can take any form, from 'embarrassing and annoying, but still mostly harmless' to 'downright devastating to your company or at least having the potential to be so'. In dealing with incidents, being prepared by applying good security practice (that is, by applying ISO27001 or other relevant standards) is half the battle. The other half consists of 'being prepared for what you can't be prepared for'. We sincerely hope that the procedures outlined in this book will help you in containing and resolving any such incidents.

ITG RESOURCES

IT Governance Ltd sources, creates and delivers products and services to meet the real-world, evolving IT governance needs of today's organizations, directors, managers and practitioners.

The ITG website (*www.itgovernance.co.uk*) is the international one-stop-shop for corporate and IT governance information, advice, guidance, books, tools, training and consultancy. On the website you will find the following pages related to information security and the subject matter of this book:

www.itgovernance.co.uk/infosec.aspx

www.itgovernance.co.uk/iso27001.aspx

Publishing Services

IT Governance Publishing (ITGP) is the world's leading IT-GRC publishing imprint that is wholly owned by IT Governance Ltd.

With books and tools covering all IT governance, risk and compliance frameworks, we are the publisher of choice for authors and distributors alike, producing unique and practical publications of the highest quality, in the latest formats available, which readers will find invaluable.

www.itgovernancepublishing.co.uk is the website dedicated to ITGP. Other titles published by ITGP that may be of interest include:

- Managing Information Security Breaches: Studies from real life

  www.itgovernance.co.uk/shop/p-923.aspx

- The True Cost of Information Security Breaches and Cyber Crime

  www.itgovernance.co.uk/shop/p-1338.aspx

- Once more unto the Breach: Managing information security in an uncertain world

  www.itgovernance.co.uk/shop/p-985.aspx.

We also offer a range of off-the-shelf *toolkits* that give comprehensive, customizable documents to help users create the specific documentation they need to properly implement a management system or standard. Written by experienced practitioners and based on the latest best practice, ITGP toolkits can save months of work for organizations working towards compliance with a given standard.

Toolkits that may be of interest include:

- ISO27001 2013 ISMS Standalone Documentation Toolkit

  www.itgovernance.co.uk/shop/p-1462.aspx

- Cyber Security Governance & Risk Management Toolkit

  www.itgovernance.co.uk/shop/p-1403.aspx

- ISO22301 Business Continuity Management System (BCMS) Implementation Toolkit

  www.itgovernance.co.uk/shop/p-1039.aspx.

Books and tools published by IT Governance Publishing (ITGP) are available from all business booksellers and the following websites:

www.itgovernance.eu *www.itgovernanceusa.com*

www.itgovernance.in *www.itgovernancesa.co.za*

www.itgovernance.asia.

Training Services

IT Governance offers an extensive portfolio of training courses designed to educate information security, IT governance, risk management and compliance professionals. Our classroom and online training programmes will help you develop the skills required to deliver best practice and compliance to your organisation.

ISO/IEC 27001:2013 is the international management Standard that helps businesses and organisations throughout the world develop a best-in-class information security management system. Knowledge and experience in implementing and maintaining ISO27001 compliance are considered to be essential to building a successful career in information security. We have the world's first programme of certificated ISO27001 education with foundation, lead implementer, risk management and lead auditor training courses. Each course is designed to provide delegates with relevant knowledge and skills and an industry-recognised qualification awarded by the International Board for IT Governance Qualifications (IBITGQ).

Full details of all IT Governance training courses can be found at *www.itgovernance.co.uk/training.aspx*.

Professional Services and Consultancy

Your mission to plug critical security gaps will be greatly assisted by IT Governance consultants, who have advised hundreds of information security managers in the adoption of ISO27001 information security management systems.

The organisation's assets, security and data systems, not to mention its reputation, are all in your hands. A major security breach could spell disaster. Timely advice and support from IT governance experts will enable you to identify the threats, assess risks and put in place the necessary controls before there's an incident.

At IT Governance, we understand that information, information security and information technology are always business issues, and not just IT ones. Our consultancy services assist you in managing information security strategies in harmony with business goals, conveying the right messages to your colleagues to support decision-making.

For more information about IT Governance consultancy, see: *www.itgovernance.co.uk/consulting.aspx*.

Newsletter

IT governance is one of the hottest topics in business today, not least because it is also the fastest moving.

You can stay up to date with the latest developments across the whole spectrum of IT governance subject matter, including; risk management, information security, ITIL® and IT service management, project governance, compliance and so much more, by subscribing to ITG's core publications and topic alert emails.

Simply visit our subscription center and select your preferences: *www.itgovernance.co.uk/newsletter.aspx*.

EU for product safety is Stephen Evans, The Mill Enterprise Hub, Stagreenan, Drogheda, Co. Louth, A92 CD3D, Ireland. (servicecentre@itgovernance.eu)

www.ingramcontent.com/pod-product-compliance
Lightning Source LLC
LaVergne TN
LVHW010546100826
845148LV00013B/2619